SECOND EDITION

CVS
Pocket Reference

Gregor N. Purdy

Beijing · Cambridge · Farnham · Köln · Paris · Sebastopol · Taipei · Tokyo

CVS Pocket Reference, Second Edition
by Gregor N. Purdy

Copyright © 2003, 2000 O'Reilly & Associates, Inc. All rights reserved. Printed in the United States of America.

Published by O'Reilly & Associates, Inc., 1005 Gravenstein Highway North, Sebastopol, CA 95472.

O'Reilly & Associates books may be purchased for educational, business, or sales promotional use. Online editions are also available for most titles (*safari.oreilly.com*). For more information, contact our corporate/institutional sales department: (800) 998-9938 or *corporate@oreilly.com*.

Editor:	Andy Oram
Production Editor:	Claire Cloutier
Cover Designer:	Hanna Dyer
Interior Designer:	David Futato

Printing History:

August 2000:	First Edition.
August 2003:	Second Edition.

0-596-00567-9
[C]

Contents

CVS Pocket Reference

Introduction

The *CVS Pocket Reference* is a quick reference guide to the Concurrent Versions System (CVS). It describes the latest version available at the time of this writing, Version 1.11.6.

Conventions Used in This Book

The following typographic conventions are used:

`Constant width`
> Indicates command-line computer output, CVS commands, and code examples.

`Constant width italic`
> Indicates variables in examples. It also indicates variables or user-defined elements within italic text (such as pathname or filenames). For instance, in the path */usr/src/directory*, replace *directory* with a directory name.

`Constant width bold`
> Indicates user input in examples.

Italic
> Introduces new terms and indicates URLs, variables in text, user-defined files and directories, commands, options, file extensions, filenames, and directory names.

↵
> Indicates code that should be typed as one line, but was set as two lines in this book, due to page width.

For More Information

The CVS home page is *http://www.cvshome.org/*.

If you have the GNU info program installed on your system, you can type info cvs to view the online documentation. For some setups, this brings up the manual page in info, and for others, it brings up more information.

The same documentation is available in PostScript form as the paper "Version Management with CVS" by Per Ceder-qvist, et al. It can be found in the CVS distribution file */usr/local/src/cvs-1.11/doc/cvs.ps*. (Of course, you need to substitute a different directory name if you've installed the distribution somewhere other than */usr/local/src*.)

Also, basic information is available by running man cvs (on Unix-like systems). Running cvs --help, cvs --help-options, and cvs --help-commands provides still more information on the specified topics. To get help on a specific command, use cvs -H *command*.

Version Control and CVS

Version control (or *revision control*) is the practice of maintaining information about a project's evolution in order to retrieve prior versions of files, track changes, and (often most importantly) coordinate the efforts of a team of developers.

The *repository* (also called an *archive*) is the centralized area that stores the projects' files, which are managed by the version control system and the repository administrator. The repository contains information required to reconstruct previous versions of the files in a project. An administrator sets up and controls the repository using procedures and commands described later in the section "CVS Administrator Reference."

A *sandbox* (also called a *working directory*) contains copies of versions of files from the repository. New development occurs in sandboxes, and any number of sandboxes can be created from a single repository. Sandboxes are independent of each other and may contain files from different development stages of the same project. Users set up and control sandboxes using the procedures and commands found in the section "CVS User Reference."

In a typical interaction with the version control system, a developer checks out the most current code from the repository, makes changes, tests the results, and commits those changes back to the repository when they are deemed satisfactory.

Locking and merging

Some systems, such as RCS (Revision Control System) and SCCS (Source Code Control System), use a *locking model* that coordinates the efforts of multiple developers by serializing file modifications. Before making changes to a file, a developer must not only obtain a copy of it but must also request and obtain a lock on it from the system. This lock serves to prevent (really, dissuade) multiple developers from working on the same file at the same time. When the changes are committed, the developer unlocks the file, permitting other developers to gain access to it.

The locking model is pessimistic: it assumes that conflicts must be avoided. Serialization of file modifications through locks prevents conflicts. However, it is cumbersome to have to lock files for editing when bug-hunting. Developers often circumvent the lock mechanism to keep working, which is an invitation to trouble.

To handle work by multiple developers on a single file, CVS uses a *merging model* that allows everyone access to the files at all times and supports concurrent development. The merging model is optimistic: it assumes that conflicts are not common and that when they do occur, it usually isn't difficult to resolve them.

CVS can operate under a locking model via the -L and -l options to the admin command. Also, CVS has special commands (edit and watch) for those who want additional development coordination support. CVS uses internal locks to prevent corruption when multiple people are accessing the repository simultaneously, but these are different from the user-visible locks of the locking model.

Conflicts and merging

If two developers commit changes to the same version of a file, CVS automatically defers the commit of the second committer's file. The second committer then issues the cvs update command, which merges the first committer's changes into the local file. In many cases, the changes are in different areas of the file, and the merge is successful. However, if both developers have made changes to the same area of the file, the second one to commit has to resolve the conflict. This involves examining the problematic areas of the file and selecting among the multiple versions or making changes that resolve the conflict.

CVS detects only textual conflicts, but conflict resolution is concerned with keeping the project as a whole logically consistent. Therefore, conflict resolution sometimes involves changing files other than the one CVS complained about.

For example, if one developer adds a parameter to a function definition, it may be necessary to make all calls to that function pass the additional parameter. This is a logical conflict, so its detection and resolution is the job of the developers (with support from tools such as compilers and debuggers); CVS won't notice the problem.

In any merge situation, whether or not there was a conflict, the second developer to commit needs to retest the resulting version of the project because it has changed since the original commit. Once it passes the test, the developer needs to recommit the file.

Tagging

CVS tracks file versions by internal revision numbers, which you can use to retrieve a particular revision from the repository. In addition, it is possible to create symbolic tags so that a group of files (or an entire project) can be referenced by a single identifier even when the revision numbers of the files are not the same (which is most often the case). This capability is often used to keep track of released versions or other important project milestones.

For example, the symbolic tag hello-1_0 might refer to revision number 1.3 of *hello.c* and revision number 1.1 of *Makefile*. Symbolic tags are created with the tag and rtag commands.

Branching

The simplest form of development is *linear*, in which there is a succession of revisions to a file, each derived from the prior revision. Many projects can get by with a completely linear development process, but larger projects (as measured by number of files, number of developers, and/or size of the user community) often run into maintenance issues that require additional capabilities. Sometimes it is desirable to do some speculative development while the main line of development continues uninterrupted. Other times, bugs in the currently released version must be fixed while work on the next version is already underway. In both cases, the solution is to create a *branch* (or *fork*) from an appropriate point in the development of the project. If, at a future time, some or all of the changes on the branch are needed on the main line of development (or elsewhere), they can be merged together (*joined*).

Branches are forked with the tag -b command; they are joined with the update -j command.

CVS Command Format

CVS commands take the form:

```
cvs global_options command command_options
```

For example, here is a simple sequence of commands showing both options in the context of creating a repository, importing existing files, and performing a few common operations on them.

Create a new repository:

```
$ cvs -d /usr/local/cvsrep init
```

Import some existing code into a new module in the repository:

```
$ cd ~/work/hello
$ cvs -d /usr/local/cvsrep import -m 'Import' hello      \
    vendor start
```

Move the old code to a backup location and check out a copy of the new module as a sandbox:

```
$ cd ..
$ mv hello hello.bak
$ cvs -d /usr/local/cvsrep checkout hello
$ cd hello
```

Change a file and commit the changes:

```
$ vi hello.c
$ cvs commit -m 'Fixed a typo'
```

Attach a symbolic tag to every file in the module:

```
$ cvs tag hello-1_0
```

Remove a file and commit the changes:

```
$ cvs remove -f Makefile
$ cvs commit -m 'Removed old Makefile'
```

Go back to the tagged version from above (*Makefile* reappears):

```
$ cvs upd -r hello-1_0
```

Go to the most recent revision of every file in the module (*Makefile* disappears again):

```
$ cvs upd -A
```

Global options apply to both user and administrator commands, and other options apply only to one or the other. The common global options are described in the next section, and the user and administrator options are described in the "CVS User Reference" section and the "CVS Administrator Reference" section, respectively.

Common Global Options

Table 1 lists common global options that apply to both user and administrator commands.

Table 1. Common global options

Option	Description
b bindir	Location of external RCS programs; this option is obsolete, having been deprecated at CVS versions above 1.9.18.
-T tempdir	Absolute path for temporary files; overrides the setting of $TMPDIR.
-v --version	Display version and copyright information.

Gotchas

This section clarifies a few aspects of CVS that sometimes cause confusion:

File orientation
   While directories are supported, they are not versioned in the same way as traditional files. This is particularly important in the early stages of a project, when the structure may be in flux. Additionally, if the project is undergoing major changes, the structure is also likely to change. See the "Hacking the Repository" section.

Text orientation
   There is no equivalent to diff for binary files, although CVS's support for binary files is usually sufficient. Use cvs admin -kb to tell CVS a file is binary.

Line orientation
> Moving a segment of code from one place in a file to another is seen as a delete (from the old location) and an unrelated add (to the new location).

Not syntax-aware
> As far as CVS is concerned, small formatting changes are equivalent to sweeping logic changes in the same line ranges.

Installing CVS

This section describes the procedure for obtaining and installing the latest distribution of CVS. The instructions assume a Unix-like operating system. Typically, if CVS is going to be intalled for shared use, the procedures given are carried out as the root user.

Only the source-based manual setup of CVS is described here, although some systems have special installation programs that allow you to download and install a binary package instead of downloading and compiling the source code yourself. Red Hat's RPM is one such package-management system.

Obtaining CVS

For versions of CVS prior to 1.11.6, releases that have one decimal point in their version numbers (such as 1.11) are the stable versions. Those with two decimal points (such as 1.11.1) are development releases.

Starting with CVS Version 1.11.6, releases that have an odd number in their minor version numbers (such as 1.11.6) are the stable versions. Those with even numbers in their minor version numbers (such as 1.12.2) are feature releases. Generally, you should use the latest stable version.

Some systems may already have an appropriate version of the CVS software installed. Check by issuing the cvs version command (or cvs -v if that doesn't work). If cvs runs, it displays its version number; if it doesn't run, it may mean that CVS is not installed or that the $PATH environment variable doesn't contain the appropriate directory. On many systems, running whereis cvs searches common installation locations regardless of the $PATH setting. If this doesn't turn up anything, try locate cvs to perform a broad search for files with "cvs" in their names. Not all systems support the locate command, so an alternative is to run·

```
find / -name cvs -print 2> /dev/null
```

to look for any files named "cvs" on your system. This command searches every directory from the root directory, so it may take a long time to complete.

To obtain a fresh copy of the desired version of CVS, simply visit the main CVS web site (*http://ccvs.cvshome.org/servlets/ ProjectDownloadList*).

Unpacking CVS

Older versions of CVS were distributed as GNU tar archives, compressed with GNU gzip (with a *.tar.gz* file extension). Newer versions are distributed as GNU tar archives, compressed with the bzip2 utility (with a *.tar.bz2* file extension). Some versions are available in both formats.

If you have GNU tar, you can use a single command to unpack CVS source distributions compressed with GNU gzip:

```
# cd /usr/local/src
# tar xvzf cvs-1.11.2.tar.gz
```

Otherwise, you need to use more commands:

```
# gunzip -c cvs-1.11.5.tar.gz | tar xvf -
```

or:

```
# bzcat cvs-1.11.6.tar.bz2 | tar xvf -
```

Whatever unpacking method you use, you are left with the directory */usr/local/src/cvs-1.11.6*, which contains the entire source distribution of CVS.

Compiling CVS

This example assumes you want to install CVS in */usr/local*:

```
# cd cvs-1.11.6
# ./configure --prefix /usr/local
# make
```

When compilation completes, you can run the CVS test suite with the command:

```
# make check
```

It can take quite a long time for the tests to complete, so if you do run the test suite, be prepared to let it run for a while before you install CVS.

Installing CVS

The make install command installs the CVS programs and documentation:

```
# make install
```

Once this is complete, other configuration steps may be necessary, such as downloading and installing the Secure Shell (ssh) or setting up your */etc/inetd.conf* or */etc/xinetd.conf* file so CVS can run in server mode. See the following section for more information.

CVS Administrator Reference

This section provides details on creating and configuring repositories and performing other CVS administrative tasks. A single computer can run multiple copies of the CVS server, and each server can serve multiple repositories.

Creating a Repository

Select a directory that will contain the repository files (*/usr/ local/cvsrep* is used in the following examples). Use the init command to initialize the repository. You can now set the $CVSROOT environment variable to the absolute path of the repository:

```
$ export CVSROOT=/usr/local/cvsrep
$ cvs init
```

You can also use the *-d* option to specify the absolute path to the repository:

```
$ cvs -d /usr/local/cvsrep init
```

For information on importing code, see the "CVS User Reference" section, especially the "import" and "add" sections.

Setting up the password server with inetd

If your server uses inetd to control services and you want users to access the repository from other computers, configure the pserver by doing the following as root:

- Make sure there is an entry in */etc/services* similar to the following:

    ```
    cvspserver 2401/tcp
    ```

- If you don't use tcpwrappers, place a line like the following in */etc/inetd.conf* (all on one line):

    ```
    cvspserver stream tcp nowait root /usr/bin/cvs cvs  ⏎
        --allow-root=/usr/local/cvsroot pserver
    ```

- If you do use tcpwrappers, place a line like this:

    ```
    cvspserver stream tcp nowait root /usr/sbin/tcpd  ⏎
        /usr/bin/cvs --allow-root=/usr/local/cvsroot pserver
    ```

- Once these changes are in place, restart inetd (or send it the appropriate signal to cause it to reread *inetd.conf*).

Setting up the password server with xinetd

If your server uses xinetd to control services and you want users to access the repository from other computers, configure the pserver by doing the following as root:

- Make sure there is a file */etc/xinetd.d/cvspserver* similar to the following:

```
service cvspserver
{
  port        = 2401
  socket_type = stream
  protocol    = tcp
  wait        = no
  user        = root
  passenv     = PATH
  server      = /usr/local/bin/cvs
  server_args = -f --allow-root=/usr/local/cvsroot ↵
    pserver
}
```

- Once these changes are in place, restart xinetd (or send it the appropriate signal to cause it to reread its configuration).

Security Issues

The following security issues need to be considered when working with CVS:

- The contents of files will be transmitted in the open over the network with pserver and rsh. With pserver, passwords are transmitted in the open as well.

- When using a local repository (i.e., when CVS is not being used in client/server mode), developers need write access to the repository, which means they can hack it.

- The CVS server runs as root briefly before changing its user ID.

- The ~/.cvspass file must be kept unreadable by all users except the owner to prevent passwords from being accessible.

- A user who has authority to make changes to the files in the *CVSROOT* module can run arbitrary programs.

- Some of the options to the admin command are very dangerous, so it is advisable to restrict its use. This can be accomplished by creating a user group named cvsadmin. If this user group exists, only users in that group can run the admin command (except admin -kkflag, which is available to everyone).

Repository Structure

The CVS repository is implemented as a normal directory with special contents. This section describes the contents of the repository directory.

The CVSROOT directory

The *CVSROOT* directory contains the administrative files for the repository; other directories in the repository contain the modules. The administrative files permit (and ignore) blank lines and comment lines in addition to the lines containing real configuration information. Comment lines start with a hash mark (#).

Some of the administrative files contain filename patterns to match file and directory names. These patterns are regular expressions such as those used in GNU Emacs. Table 2 contains the special constructions used most often.

Table 2. Filename pattern special constructions

Construction	Description
^	Match the beginning of the string.
$	Match the end of the string.
.	Match any single character.
*	Modify the preceding construct to match zero or more repetitions.

CVS performs a few important expansions in the contents of the administrative files before interpreting the results. First, the typical shell syntax for referring to a home directory is ~/, which expands to the home directory of the user running CVS; ~*user* expands to the home directory of the specified user.

In addition, CVS provides a mechanism similar to the shell's environment variable expansion capability. Constructs such as ${*variable*} are replaced by the value of the named variable. Variable names start with letters and consist entirely of letters, numbers, and underscores. Curly brackets may be omitted if the character immediately following the variable reference is not a valid variable name character. While this construct looks like a shell environment variable reference, the full environment is not available. Table 3 contains the built-in variables.

Table 3. Administrative file variables

Variable	Description
CVSEDITOR EDITOR VISUAL	The editor CVS uses for log file editing.
CVSROOT	The repository locator in use.
USER	The name of the user (on the server, if using a remote repository) running CVS.
=*var*	The value of a user-defined variable named *var*; values for these variables are provided by the global *-s* option.

To edit the administrative files, check out the *CVSROOT* module from the repository, edit the files, and commit them back to the repository. You must commit the changes for them to affect CVS's behavior.

Table 4 describes the administrative files and their functions.

Table 4. CVSROOT files

File	Description
checkoutlist	Extra files to be maintained in *CVSROOT*.
commitinfo	Specifications for commit governors.
config	Settings to affect the behavior of CVS.
cvsignore	Filename patterns of files to ignore.
cvswrappers	Specifications for `checkout` and `commit` filters.
editinfo	Specifications for log editors (obsolete).
history	Log information for the `history` command.
loginfo	Specify `commit` notifier program(s).
modules	Module definitions.
notify	Notification processing specifications.
passwd	A list of users and their CVS-specific passwords.
rcsinfo	Template form for log messages.
readers	A list of users having read-only access.
taginfo	Tag processing specifications.
users	Alternate user email addresses for use with *notify*.
verifymsg	Specify log message evaluator program.
writers	A list of users having read/write access.

Because the *editinfo* file is obsolete, use the $EDITOR environment variable (or the *-e* option) to specify the editor and the *verifymsg* file to specify an evaluator.

Each line of the *taginfo* file contains a filename pattern and a command line to execute when files with matching names are tagged.

The checkoutlist file

Whenever changes to files in the *CVSROOT* module are committed, CVS displays the message:

```
cvs commit: Rebuilding administrative file database
```

This informs you that the checked-out copy in the repository has been updated to reflect any changes just committed. As with any other module directory in the repository, the *CVSROOT* directory contains RCS (*,v) files that retain the history of the files. However, to use the files, CVS needs a copy of the latest revision. So, when CVS displays this message, it is checking out the latest revisions of the administrative files.

If you have added files to the *CVSROOT* module (such as scripts to be called via entries in the *loginfo* file), you will need to list them in the *checkoutlist* file. This makes CVS treat them the same way it treats the standard set of *CVSROOT* files.

Each line in this file consists of a filename and an optional error message that displays in case there is trouble checking out the file.

The commitinfo file

Whenever a `commit` is processed, CVS consults the *commitinfo* file to determine whether or not any precommit checking of the file is required. Each line of the file contains a directory name pattern, followed by the path of a program to invoke when files are commited in directories with matching names.

Aside from the usual filename-pattern syntax, there are two special patterns:

ALL
> If this pattern is present in the file, all files are passed to the specified checking program. CVS then looks for a pattern that matches the name of each particular file and runs the additional checks found, if any.

DEFAULT
> If this pattern is present in the file, all files for which there was no pattern match are sent to the specified checking program. The automatic match of every file to

the ALL entry, if any, does not count as a match when determining whether or not to send the file to the DEFAULT checking program.

CVS constructs the command line for the checking program by appending the full path to the directory within the repository and the list of files being committed (this means you can specify the first few command-line arguments to the program, if necessary). If the checking program exits with a non-zero status, the commit is aborted.

The programs that run via this mechanism run on the server computer when a remote repository is used. Here is an example of a *commitinfo* file:

```
ALL $CVSROOT/CVSROOT/commit-ALL.pl
DEFAULT $CVSROOT/CVSROOT/commit-DEFAULT.pl
CVSROOT$ $CVSROOT/CVSROOT/commit-CVSROOT.pl
```

This example assumes you will create the script files in the *CVSROOT* module and add them to the *checkoutlist* file.

The config file

Repository configuration is specified in the *config* administrative file. Entries can be:

LockDir=*dir*

Directs CVS to put its lock files in the alternate directory given instead of in the repository itself, allowing users without write access to the repository (but with write access to *dir*) to read from the repository.

Version 1.11 supports this option. Version 1.10 doesn't support alternate directories for lock files and reports an error if this option is set. Older versions of CVS (1.9 and previous) don't support this option either and will not report an error. Do not mix versions that support alternate directories for lock files with versions that don't, because lock files in both places defeat the purpose of having them.

LogHistory=*types*

> Determines the types of activities that are logged to the *history* administrative file. The special value all implies all the record types listed in Tables 27, 28, and 29. Any subset of those record types can be specified by listing them. For example, the line LogHistory=MAR logs only events related to commits.

SystemAuth=*value*

> CVS tries to authenticate users via the *CVSROOT/passwd* file first; if that fails and this option is set to yes, CVS tries to authenticate via the system's user database. This option is used with the password server. The default is yes.

TopLevelAdmin=*value*

> If this option is set to yes, an additional *CVS* directory is created at the top-level directory when checkout is run. This allows the client software to detect the repository locator in that directory (see the "Repository Locators" section). The default is no.
>
> This option is useful if you check out multiple modules to the same sandbox directory. If it is enabled, you don't have to provide a repository locator after the first checkout; CVS infers it from the information in the top-level *CVS* directory created during the first checkout.

The cvsignore file

The *cvsignore* administrative file contains a list of filename patterns to ignore, just like the *.cvsignore* files that can appear in sandboxes and user home directories. Unlike the filename patterns in most other administrative files, these patterns are in sh syntax; they are not GNU Emacs-style regular expressions. There can be multiple patterns on a line, separated by whitespace (consequently, the patterns themselves cannot contain whitespace).

There is a slight difference between filename patterns in sh and CVS. Because the CVS patterns are not subject to variable interpolation, a pattern such as _$* (which is one of the patterns built into CVS) matches a file named _$foo but not one named _. But, if you present the same pattern to a shell, it interprets the $* part as a shell variable and tries to expand it, resulting probably in an empty string. Thus, $* in a shell matches only the one-character filename _, not _$foo. This becomes particularly important if you write your own utilities to work with CVS and need to implement the same policy for ignoring files.

Table 5 shows the most commonly used sh-style pattern constructs.

Table 5. Filename patterns for cvsignore

Construct	Description
?	Any one character.
*	Any sequence of zero or more characters.

Again, diverging from the standards used by the rest of the administrative files, the *cvsignore* file does not support comments.

The cvswrappers file

While the *cvsignore* file allows CVS to ignore certain files, the *cvswrappers* file allows you to give CVS default options for commands that work with files. Lines in this file consist of a sh-style filename pattern followed by a -k (keyword substitution mode) option and/or an -m (update method) option. The legal values for -k are described in Table 19. The legal values for -m are COPY and MERGE.

If -m COPY is specified, CVS doesn't attempt to merge the files. Instead, it presents the user with conflicting versions of the file, and the user can choose one or the other or can resolve the conflict manually.

For example, to treat all files ending in *.jpg* as binary, add this line to the file:

```
*.jpg -k b
```

The history file

If the *history* file exists, CVS stores records of repository activity in it. This information is used in the displays of the `cvs history` command. The *history* file is not intended for direct reading or writing by programs other than CVS.

A repository set up with `cvs init` automatically has a *history* file.

The loginfo file

The *loginfo* administrative file works much like the *commitinfo* file and can use the special patterns ALL and DEFAULT. This file allows you to process commit log messages and related information.

The programs called during *loginfo* processing receive the log message on standard input. Table 6 shows the three codes that can pass additional information to the called programs via command-line arguments.

Table 6. Special loginfo variables

Variable	Description
s	Filename.
V	Precommit revision number.
v	Post-commit revision number.

If a percent sign (%) followed by the desired variable is placed after the command path, CVS inserts the corresponding information as a whitespace-separated list with one entry for each file, preceded by the repository path (as with *commitinfo*). There can be only one percent sign on the command line, so if you want information from more than one variable, place the variable names inside curly brackets: %{...}. In this case, each file-specific entry has one field for each variable, separated by commas. For example, the code %{sVv} expands to a list like this:

```
/usr/local/cvsrep/hello Makefile,1.1,1.2 hello.c,1.8,1.9
```

It can be helpful to send email notifications each time someone commits a file to the repository. Developers can monitor this stream of notices to determine when they should pull the latest development code into their private sandboxes. For example, consider a developer doing some preparatory work in his sandbox while he awaits stabilization and addition of another developer's new library. As soon as the new library is added and committed, email notification goes out, and the waiting developer sees that the code is ready to use. So, he runs cvs upd -d in the appropriate directory to pull in the new library code and then sets about integrating it with his work.

It is simple to set up this kind of notification. Just add a line like this to the *CVSROOT/loginfo* file:

```
DEFAULT mail -s %s developers@company.com
```

Often, the email address is a mailing list that has all the interested parties (developers or otherwise) on the distribution list. If you want to send messages to multiple email addresses, you can write a script to do that and have that script called via this file. Alternatively, you can use the *log.pl* program that comes as part of the CVS source distribution (located at */usr/local/src/cvs-1.11/contrib/log.pl*, assuming CVS was unpacked into */usr/local/src*). Instructions for its use are provided as comments in the file.

The modules file

The top-level directories in a repository are called *modules*. In addition to these physical modules, CVS provides a mechanism to create logical modules through the *modules* administrative file. Here are the three kinds of logical modules:

Alias

Alias modules are defined by lines of the form:

```
module_name -a alias_module …
```

Using an alias module name in a CVS command is equivalent to using its component modules (after the -a option in the previous code example) directly.

Regular

Regular modules are defined by lines of the form:

```
module_name [options] directory file …
```

Checking out *module_name* results in the specified files from *directory* being checked out into a directory named *module_name*. The intervening directories (if any) are not reflected in the sandbox.

Ampersand

Ampersand modules are defined by lines of the form:

```
module_name [options] &other_module …
```

Checking out such a module results in a directory named *module_name*, which in turn contains copies of the *other_module* modules.

Table 7 shows the options that can define modules.

Table 7. Module options

Option	Description
-d name	Override the default working directory name for the module.
-e prog	Run the program *prog* when files are exported from the module; the module name is passed to *prog* as the sole argument.
-i prog	Run the program *prog* when files are committed to the module; the repository directory of the committed files is passed to *prog* as the sole argument.
-i prog	Run the program *prog* when files are checked out from the module; the module name is passed to *prog* as the sole argument.

Table 7. Module options (continued)

Option	Description
-s *status*	Assign a status descriptor to the module.
-t *prog*	Run the program *prog* when files are tagged in the module using rtag; the module name and the symbolic tag are passed to *prog*.
-u *prog*	Run the program *prog* when files are updated in the module's top-level directory; the full path to the module within the repository is passed to *prog* as the sole argument.

Alias modules provide alternative names for other modules or shortcuts that refer to collections or subdirectories of other modules. Alias-module definitions function like macro definitions in that they cause commands to run as if the expanded list of modules and directories was on the command line. Alias modules do not cause the modules of their definition to be grouped together under the alias name (use ampersand modules for that). For example, the definition:

```
h -a hello
```

makes the name *h* a synonym for the *hello* module. This definition:

```
project -a library client server
```

allows you to check out all three modules of the project as a unit. If an entry in the definition of an alias module is preceded by an exclamation point (!), the named directory is excluded from the module.

Regular modules allow you to create modules that are subsets of other modules. For example, the definition:

```
header library library.h
```

creates the *header* module that contains just the *library.h* file from the *library* module.

Ampersand modules are true logical modules. There are no top-level directories for them in the repository, but you can check them out to sandboxes, and directories with their names will then appear. The modules listed in the definition are below that directory. For example:

```
project &library &client &server
```

is almost the same as the alias module example given earlier, except that the submodules are checked out inside a subdirectory named *project*.

In this file, long definitions may be split across multiple lines by terminating all but the last line with backslashes (\).

The notify file

This file is used in conjunction with the watch command. When notifications are appropriate, this file is consulted to determine how to do the notification.

Each line of the *notify* file contains a filename pattern and a command line. CVS's notification mechanism uses the command line specified to perform notifications for files with names that match the corresponding pattern.

There is a single special-purpose variable, %s, that can appear in the command specification. When the command is executed, the name of the user to notify replaces the variable name. If the *users* administrative file exists, the usernames are looked up there, and the resulting values are used for %s instead. This allows emails to be sent to accounts other than those on the local machine. Details are sent to the notification program via standard input.

Typical usage of this feature is the single entry:

```
ALL mail %s -s "CVS notification"
```

In fact, this entry is present in the default *notify* file created when you run cvs init to create a repository (although it is initially commented out).

The passwd file

If you access the repository via a pserver repository locator (see the "Repository Locators" section), CVS can have its own private authentication information, separate from the system's user database. This information is stored in the *CVSROOT/passwd* administrative file.

This feature provides anonymous CVS access over the Internet. By creating an entry for a public user (usually anoncvs or anonymous), the pserver can be used by many people sharing the public account. If you don't want to create a system user with the same name as the public user or if you have such a user but it has a different purpose, you can employ a user alias to map it to something else:

```
anonymous:TY7QWpLw8bvus:cvsnoname
```

Then, make sure you create the cvsnoname user on the system. You can use */bin/false* as the login shell and the repository's root directory as the home directory for the user.

If you leave the password field empty for the anonymous user, CVS will accept any password (as of Version 1.11). To restrict the public user to read-only access, list it in the *CVSROOT/readers* administrative file.

Additionally, CVS's private user database is useful even if you don't want to set up anonymous CVS access. You can restrict access to a subset of the system's users, provide remote access to users who don't have general system access, or prevent a user's normal system password from being transmitted in the clear over the network (see the "Security Issues" section).

There is no cvs passwd command for setting CVS-specific passwords (located in the repository file *CVSROOT/passwd*). CVS-specific user and password management is a manual task.

The rcsinfo file

CVS consults this file when doing a commit or import to determine the log message editor template. Each entry in the file consists of a filename pattern and the name of the file to use as the template for module directories with matching names.

The ALL and DEFAULT special patterns apply to this file.

The readers file

If this file exists, users listed in it have read-only access.

The taginfo file

CVS consults this file whenever the tag or rtag commands are used. Entries in this file are filename patterns and program specifications. The ALL special pattern applies to this file.

The programs specified in the *taginfo* file are called with the tag, the operation being performed, the module directory name (relative to the repository root), and the filename and revision number for each affected file. The valid operations are add (for tag), del (for tag -d), and mov (for tag -F).

If a program specified in the *taginfo* file returns a nonzero status, the tag or rtag command that caused its execution is aborted.

The users file

If this file exists, it is consulted during processing of the *notify* administrative file's contents. Entries in this file consist of two colon-separated fields on a single line. The first field is the name of a user, and the second field is a value (normally the user's email address on another machine). For example:

```
john:john@somecompany.com
jane:jane@anothercompany.com
```

The verifymsg file

CVS consults this file to determine if log messages should be validated. If the program returns a nonzero status, the commit is aborted. The *verifymsg* file is called with the full path to a file containing the log message to be verified.

The ALL special pattern is not supported for this file, although DEFAULT is. If more than one pattern matches, the first match is used.

The writers file

If this file exists, users listed in it have read/write access (unless they are also listed in the *readers* file, in which case they have read-only access).

Hacking the Repository

Because the repository is a normal directory, albeit one with special contents, it is possible to cd into the directory and examine its contents and/or make changes to the files and directories there. For each file that has been added there will be a file with the same name followed by ,v in a corresponding directory in the repository. These are RCS (the format, not the program) files that contain multiple versions of the file.

WARNING

Because the activities discussed in this section involve making changes directly to the repository instead of working through CVS commands, you should exercise extreme caution and have current backups when following these instructions.

Restructuring a project

Restructuring the project by moving files and directories around (and possibly renaming them) in the repository allows the files to retain their history. The standard way to rename a file when using CVS is to rename the file in the sandbox and do a cvs remove on the old name and a cvs add on the new name. This results in the file being disconnected from its history under the new name, so sometimes it is better to do the renaming directly in the repository. However, doing this while people have active sandboxes is dangerous, because the sandboxes contain information about a file that is no longer in the repository.

Removing unwanted files

When importing an entire project, all the project's files are added to the repository; however, if some of these files shouldn't be added, you'll want to remove them. Doing a cvs remove accomplishes this, but copies of those files will remain in the repository's *.Attic* directory forever. To avoid this, you can delete the files from the repository directly before checking out sandboxes from it.

Importing

If you have an existing code base, you'll want to import it into CVS in a way that preserves the most historical information. This section provides instructions for importing projects into CVS from code snapshots or other version control systems. Except for the code snapshot import procedure, all of these are based on conversion to RCS files, followed by placing the RCS files in the proper location in the CVS repository.

Importing code snapshots

If you maintain project history archives manually by taking periodic snapshots of the code, you can import the first snapshot, tag it with the date or version number, and then successively overlay the updated files from later archives. Each set can then be committed and tagged in order to bootstrap a repository that maintains the prior history.

For example, first unpack the distributions (this assumes they unpack to directories containing the version numbers):

```
$ tar xvzf foo-1.0.tar.gz
$ tar xvzf foo-1.1.tar.gz
$ tar xvzf foo-2.0.tar.gz
```

Next, make a copy of the first version, import it into the CVS repository, check it out to make a sandbox (because importing doesn't convert the source directory into a sandbox), and use cvs tag to give it a symbolic name reflecting the project version:

```
$ mkdir foo
$ cp -R -p foo-1.0/* foo
$ cd foo
$ cvs import -m 'Imported version 1.0' foo vendor start
$ cd ..
$ mv foo foo.bak
$ cvs checkout foo
$ cd foo
$ cvs tag foo-1_0
$ cd ..
```

Now, apply the differences between Version 1.0 and 1.1 to the sandbox, commit the changes, and create a tag:

```
$ diff -Naur foo-1.0 foo-1.1 | (cd foo; patch -Np1)
$ cd foo
$ cvs commit -m 'Imported version 1.1'
$ cvs tag foo-1_1
$ cd ..
```

After the cd foo step, you might have to deal with added or removed files, which you can detect by looking at the output of cvs -n -q upd -AdP. If you have added or removed files in the snapshot just applied, you can issue cvs remove *file* and cvs add *file* so that when you do the cvs commit, not only will the modified files have their changes committed, but the new files will get added and the old files will get removed.

Finally, apply the differences between Version 1.1 and 2.0 to the sandbox, commit the changes, and create a tag:

```
$ diff -Naur foo-1.1 foo-2.0 | (cd foo; patch -Np1)
$ cd foo
$ cvs commit -m 'Imported version 2.0'
$ cvs tag foo-2_0
```

You can now use the log command to view the history of the files, browse past versions of the files, and continue development under version control.

Importing from RCS

If you migrate from RCS to CVS, following these instructions results in a usable CVS repository. This procedure involves direct modification of the CVS repository, so it should be undertaken with caution.

Before beginning, make sure none of the files to be imported into CVS are locked by RCS. Then, create a new CVS repository and module (or a new module within an existing repository). Next, create directories in the CVS repository to mirror the project's directory structure. Finally, copy all the version files (*,v*) from the project (which may be in *RCS* subdirectories) into the appropriate directories in the repository (without *RCS* subdirectories).

For example, first move aside the directory under RCS control, create an empty directory to build the new CVS structure, import the directory, and then check it out to make a sandbox:

```
$ mv foo foo-rcs
$ mkdir foo
$ cd foo
$ cvs import -m 'New empty project' foo vendor start
$ cd ..
$ mv foo foo.bak
$ cvs checkout foo
```

Next, make directories and add them to the repository to match the structure in the RCS project:

```
$ cd foo
$ mkdir dir
$ cvs add dir
$ cd ..
```

Now, copy the *,v* files from the RCS project into the repository for the CVS project:

```
$ cp -p foo-rcs/*,v $CVSROOT/foo
$ cp -p foo-rcs/dir/*,v $CVSROOT/foo/dir
```

Finally, issue the cvs update command in the sandbox directory to bring in the latest versions of all the files:

```
$ cd foo
$ cvs upd
```

Importing from SCCS

To import from SCCS, use the *sccs2rcs* script located in the *contrib* directory of the CVS distribution to convert the files to RCS format, and then follow the preceding RCS procedure. You must have both CVS and SCCS installed for this to work. The script's comments contain additional instructions.

Importing from PVCS

To import from PVCS, use the *pvcs_to_rcs* script located in the *contrib* directory of the CVS distribution to convert the files to RCS format, and then follow the preceding RCS procedure. You must have both CVS and PVCS installed for this to work. The script's comments contain additional instructions.

Using an Interim Shared Sandbox

Over time, projects will sometimes develop unintended environmental dependencies, especially when there is no pressure for the code to be relocatable. A project developed outside version control may even be initially developed in-place (at its intended installation location). While these practices are not recommended, they do occur in real-world situations. CVS can help improve the situation by encouraging relocatability from the beginning of a project.

The default mode of operation for CVS is multiple independent sandboxes, all coordinated with a central shared repository. Code that runs in this environment is necessarily (at least partially) relocatable. So, using CVS from the beginning of a project helps ensure flexibility.

However, if a project is already well underway, an interim approach can be used. For example, you can convert the development area to a single shared sandbox by importing the code into CVS and checking it back out again:

```
$ cd /usr/local/bar
$ cvs import bar vendor start
$ cd ..
$ mv bar bar.bak
$ cvs checkout bar
```

Chances are good that this approach is too aggressive and will check in more files than absolutely necessary. You can either go back and hack the repository to remove the files that shouldn't be there or just issue the cvs remove command to delete them as you discover them.

In addition, there will probably be some binary files in the sandbox that were imported as text files. Wherever you see a binary file that needs to remain in the repository, you should issue the command cvs admin -kb *file*, then make a fresh copy from the project backup. Finally, issue the command cvs commit *file* to commit the fixed file back to the repository.

Having version control in place before making flexibility enhancements is a good idea, because it makes it easier to find (and possibly reverse) changes that cause trouble.

The repository locator (see the "Repository Locators" section) is specified via the -d option or the $CVSROOT environment variable. It is stored in the various *CVS/root* sandbox files. If you use the password server (pserver), the user ID of the person checking out the sandbox is retained. If more than one person is working with a particular sandbox, they will have to share an account for CVS access.

One way to do this is to have a neutral user account with a password known to everyone with CVS access. One person then issues the cvs login command with that user ID and password. Once you stop using a shared sandbox, this workaround won't be necessary. However, while you're using a shared sandbox, it's important that the developers type their real user IDs into their log messages, because all the changes will appear to be made by the common user.

Global Server Option

The server has one global option, --allow-root=*rootdir*. This option tells the CVS server to accept and process requests for the specified repository.

Administrator Commands

Table 8 lists the commands CVS administrators use to manage their repositories.

Table 8. Administrator commands

Command	Description
admin adm rcs	Perform administrative functions.
init	Create a new repository.
kserver	Run in Kerberos server mode.
pserver	Run in password server mode.
server	Run in remote server mode.

admin

```
admin
    [ -b[rev] ]
    [ -cstring ]
    [ -kkflag ]
    [ -l[rev] ]
    [ -L ]
```

```
[ -mrev:msg ]
[ -nname[:[rev]] ]
[ -Nname[:[rev]] ]
[ -orange ]
[ -q ]
[ -sstate[:rev] ]
[ -t[file] ]
[ -t-string ]
[ -u[rev] ]
[ -U ]
[ files … ]
```

The admin command performs administrative functions. If a
cvsadmin user group exists, only the users in that group can
run admin with options other than -k. Additional options that
may be used with the admin command are listed in Table 9.

Table 9. admin options

Option	Description
-b[rev]	Set the default branch.
-cstring	Obsolete; set the comment leader.
-kkflag	Set the default keyword substitution mode.
-l[rev]	Lock the specified revision.
-L	Enable strict locking.
-mrev:msg	Change the revision's log message.
-nname[:[rev]]	Give the specified branch or revision the symbolic name *name*.
-Nname[:[rev]]	The same as -n, except that if *name* is already in use, it is moved.
-orange	Delete revisions permanently.
-q	Don't display diagnostics.
-sstate[:rev]	Change the state of a revision.
-t[file]	Set the descriptive text in the RCS file.
-t-string	Set the descriptive text in the RCS file to *string*.
-u[rev]	Unlock the specified revision.
-U	Disable strict locking.

If the revision specified for *-l* is a branch, the latest revision on that branch will be used. If no revision is given, the latest revision on the default branch is used.

If the name given for *-n* is already in use, an error is generated. You can use *-N* to move a tag (change the revision associated with the tag); however, you should use cvs tag or cvs rtag instead.

The *-o* option is dangerous and results in a permanent loss of information from the repository. Use it with extreme caution and only after careful consideration. See Table 10 for the various ways to specify ranges. There must not be any branches or locks on the revisions to be removed. Beware of interactions between this command and symbolic names.

Table 10. Range formats

Format	Description
rev1::rev2	Eliminate versions between rev1 and rev2, retaining only enough information to go directly from rev1 to rev2; the two specified versions are retained.
::rcv2	The same as rev1::rev2, except the first revision is the branchpoint revision.
rev1::	The same as rev1::rev2, except the second revision is the end of the branch, and it is deleted instead of retained.
rev	Delete the specified revision.
rev1:rev2	The same as rev1::rev2, except the two named revisions are deleted as well.
:rev2	The same as ::rev2, except the named revision is deleted as well.
rev1:	The same as rev1::, except the named revision is deleted as well.

If no *file* is specified for the *-t* option, CVS reads from standard input until it reaches the end of the file or a period on a line by itself.

The determination of the target revision for the *-u* option is the same as for *-l*.

The options in Table 11 are present in CVS for historical reasons and should not be used. (Using these options may corrupt the repository.)

Table 11. Obsolete admin options

Option	Description
-alogins	Append the logins to the RCS file's access list.
-Aoldfile	Append the access list of *oldfile* to the access list of the RCS file.
-e[logins]	Erase logins from the RCS file's access list, or erase all if a list is not provided.
-i	Create and initialize a new RCS file. Instead of this option, use add to add files to a CVS repository.
-l	Run interactively; this option doesn't work with client/server CVS and is likely to be removed in a future version.
-Vn	Specify that the RCS files used by CVS should be made compatible with a specific version of RCS.
-xsuffixes	Determine the filename suffix for RCS files; however, CVS has always used only *,v* as the RCS file suffix.

init

```
init
```

The init command initializes the repository. Use the global *-d* option to specify the repository's directory if $CVSROOT isn't set appropriately.

The newly initialized repository contains a *CVSROOT* module and nothing else. Once the repository is initialized, use other CVS commands to add files to it or to check out the *CVSROOT* module to make changes to the administrative files.

kserver

```
kserver
```

This command operates as a server with Kerberos authentication, providing access to the repositories specified before the command with the --allow-root option. This command is used in the *inetd.conf* file, not on the command line. Another global option frequently used with this command is -T (see Table 1).

pserver

```
pserver
```

This command operates as a password-authenticated server, providing access to the repositories specified before the command with the --allow-root option. This command is used in the *inetd.conf* file, not on the command line. Another global option frequently used with this command is T (see Table 1).

server

```
server
```

The CVS client runs this command on the remote machine when connecting to a repository specified by an :ext: repository locator (usually via RSH or SSH).

CVS User Reference

This section provides details on connecting to a repository, the structure of sandboxes, and using CVS commands.

Repository Locators

CVS currently supports six methods for the client to access the repository: local, forked, external, a password server, a GSS-API (Generic Security Services API) server, and a Kerberos

4 server (most Kerberos users will want to use GSS-API). Table 12 describes the various repository locator types and their respective access methods.

Table 12. Repository access types and methods

Method	Locator format	Description
Local	*path* :local:*path*	If the repository directory is local to the computer from which you will access it (or appears local, such as an NFS- or Samba-mounted filesystem), the repository string is just the pathname of the repository directory, such as */usr/local/cvsrep*, or it can use the :local: prefix.
Forked local	:fork:*path*	This type of locator is used primarily for debugging the CVS protocol code, because it causes CVS to start (fork) a separate process to work with the repository and communicates with it using the CVS remote protocol.
External	:ext:*user@host: path*	External repositories are accessed via a remote shell utility, usually rsh (the default) or ssh. The environment variable $CVS_RSH specifies the remote shell program.
Password server	:pserver: *user@host:path*	Password server repositories require authentication to a user account before you can use the repository. Public CVS servers are commonly configured this way so they can provide anonymous CVS access. See "The passwd file" section earlier in this chapter for more information on anonymous CVS.
GSS-API server	:gserver:	This locator type is used for servers accessible via Kerberos 5 or other authentication mechanisms supported by GSS-API.
Kerberos server	:kserver:	This locator type is used for servers accessible via Kerberos 4.

Configuring CVS

CVS's behavior can be influenced by two classes of settings other than the command-line arguments: *environment variables* (see Table 13) and *special files* (see Table 14).

Table 13. Environment variables

Variable	Description
$CVS_CLIENT_LOG	Client-side debugging file specification for client/server connections. $CVS_CLIENT_LOG is the basename for the *$CVS_CLIENT_LOG.in* and *$CVS_CLIENT_LOG.out* files, which are written in the current working directory at the time a command is executed.
$CVS_CLIENT_PORT	The port number for :kserver: locators. $CVS_CLIENT_PORT doesn't need to be set if the kserver is listening on port 1999 (the default).
$CVS_IGNORE_REMOTE_ROOT	According to the change log, this variable was removed from CVS with Version 1.10.3.
$CVS_PASSFILE	Password file for :pserver: locators. This variable must be set before issuing the cvs login to have the desired effect. Defaults to *$HOME/.cvspass*.
$CVS_RCMD_PORT	For non-Unix clients, the port for connecting to the server's rcmd daemon.
$CVS_RSH	Remote shell for :ext: locators, if not rsh.
$CVS_SERVER	Remote server program for :ext: locators, if not cvs.
$CVS_SERVER_SLEEP	Server-side execution delay (in seconds) to allow time to attach a debugger.
$CVSEDITOR	Editor used for log messages; overrides $EDITOR.
$CVSIGNORE	A list of filename patterns to ignore, separated by whitespace. (See also *cvsignore* in Table 4 and *.cvsignore* in Table 14.)
$CVSREAD	Determines read-only (if the variable is set) or read/write (if the variable is not set) for checkout and update.
$CVSROOT	Default repository locator.

Table 13. Environment variables (continued)

Variable	Description
$CVSUMASK	Determines permissions for (local) repository files.
$CVSWRAPPERS	A list of filename patterns for the *cvswrappers* function. See also the "Repository Structure." section.
$EDITOR	Specifies the editor to use for log messages; see notes for $CVSEDITOR.
$HOME	On Unix, used to find the *.cvsrc* file.
$HOMEDRIVE	On Windows NT, used to find the *.cvsrc* file.
$HOMEPATH	On Windows NT, used to find the *.cvsrc* file.
$PATH	Used to locate programs to run.
$TEMP $TMP $TMPDIR	Location for temporary files. $TMPDIR is used by the server. On Unix, */tmp* (and TMP on Windows NT) may not be overridden for some functions of CVS due to reliance on the system's tmpnam( ) function.
$VISUAL	Specifies the editor to use for log messages; see notes for $CVSEDITOR.

Despite the similarity in names, the $CVSROOT environment variable and the *CVSROOT* directory in a repository are not related to each other.

The "RSH" in the name of the $CVS_RSH environment variable doesn't refer to the particular program (rsh), but rather to the program CVS is supposed to use to create remote shell connections (which can be some program other than rsh, such as ssh).

Because there is only one way to specify the remote shell program to use ($CVS_RSH) and because this is a global setting, users that commonly access multiple repositories may need to pay close attention to which repository they are using. If one repository requires one setting of this variable and another requires a different setting, you have to change this variable between accesses to repositories requiring different settings. This aspect of the repository access method is not stored in the *CVS/Root* file in the sandbox (see the section "CVS directories"). For example, if you access some repositories via rsh and some via ssh, you can create the following two utility aliases (bash syntax):

```
$ alias cvs="export CVS_RSH=ssh; cvs"
$ alias cvr="export CVS_RSH=rsh; cvs"
```

Table 14 shows the files used by the CVS command-line client for server connection and client configuration information. These files reside in the user's home directory.

Table 14. Client configuration files

Option	Description
~/.cvsignore	Filename patterns of files to ignore.
~/.cvspass	Passwords cached by cvs login.
~/.cvsrc	Default command options.
~/.cvswrappers	User-specific checkout and commit filters.

The ~/.*cvspass* file is really an operational file, not a configuration file. It is used by the cvs client program to store the repository user account password between cvs login and cvs logoff.

Here are two common .*cvsrc* settings are:

update -dP
    Bring in new directories and prune empty directories on cvs update

diff -c
    Give output in context diff format

Creating a Sandbox

In order to use CVS, you must create a sandbox or have one created for you. This section describes the steps to sandbox creation, assuming there is already a module in the repository you want to work with. See the import command in the

"User Commands" section for information on importing a new module into the repository.

1. Determine the repository locator. Talk to the repository administrator if you need help finding the repository or getting the locator syntax right.
2. If this will be your main repository, set $CVSROOT; otherwise, use the *-d* option when running CVS commands that don't infer the repository from the sandbox files.
3. Pick a module to check out.
4. Pick a sandbox location and cd to the parent directory.
5. If the repository requires login, do cvs login.
6. Run cvs checkout *module*.

For example:

```
$ export CVSROOT=/usr/local/cvsroot
$ cd ~/work
$ cvs checkout hello
```

Sandbox Structure

This section describes the files and directories that may be encountered in sandboxes.

.cvsignore files

Sandboxes may contain *.cvsignore* files. These files specify filename patterns for files that may exist in the sandbox but that normally won't be checked into CVS. This is commonly used to cause CVS to bypass derived files.

.cvswrappers files

Sandboxes may contain *.cvswrappers* files, which provide directory-specific file handling information like that in the repository configuration file *cvswrappers*.

CVS directories

Each directory in a sandbox contains a *CVS* directory. The files in this directory (see Table 15) contain metadata used by CVS to locate the repository and track which file versions have been copied into the sandbox.

Table 15. Files in the CVS directories

File	Description
Base *Baserev* *Baserev.tmp*	The *Base* directory stores copies of files when the edit command is in use. The *Baserev* file contains the revision numbers of the files in *Base*. The *Baserev.tmp* file is used to update the *Baserev* file.
Checkin.prog *Update.prog*	The programs specified in the *modules* file for options -*i* and -*u*, respectively (if any).
Entries	Version numbers and timestamps for the files as they were copied from the repository when checked out or updated.
Entries.Backup *Entries.Log* *Entries.Static*	Temporary and intermediate files used by CVS.
Notify *Notify.tmp*	Temporary files used by CVS for dealing with notifications for commands such as edit and unedit.
Repository	The name by which the directory is known in the repository.
Root	The repository locator in effect when the sandbox was created (via cvs checkout).
Tag	Information about sticky tags and dates for files in the directory.
Template	Used to store the contents of the *rcsinfo* administrative file from the repository for remote repositories.

Because each sandbox directory has one *CVS/Root* file, a sandbox directory corresponds to exactly one repository. You cannot check out some files from one repository and some from another into a single sandbox directory.

Client Global Options

Table 16 lists the global options that control the operation of the CVS client program.

Table 16. Client global options

Option	Description
-a	Authenticate (gserver only).
-d root	Locate the repository. Overrides the setting of $CVSROOT.
-e editor	Specify message editor. Overrides the settings of $CVSEDITOR and $EDITOR.
-f	Don't read ~/.cvsrc. Useful when you have .cvsrc settings that you want to forgo for a particular command.
-H [command] --help [command]	Display help. If no command is specified, displays general CVS help, including a list of other help options.
-l	Don't log command in history.
-n	Don't change any files. Useful when you want to know ahead of time which files will be affected by a particular command.
-q	Be quiet.
-Q	Be very quiet. Display messages for serious problems only.
-r	Make new working files read-only.
-s variable=value	Set the value of a user variable to a given value. User variables can be used in the contents of administrative files.
-t	Trace execution. Helpful in debugging remote repository connection problems and, in conjunction with -n, in determining the effect of an unfamiliar command.
-w	Make new working files read/write. Overrides $CVSREAD. Files are read/write unless $CVSREAD is set or -r is specified.
-x	Encrypt. (Introduced in Version 1.10.)
-z gzip_level	Set the compression level. Useful when using CVS in client/server mode across slow connections.

Common Client Options

Tables 17 and 18 describe the options that are common to many CVS commands. Table 17 lists the common options with a description of their function, while Table 18 lists which options can be used with the user commands. In the sections that follow, details are provided only for options that are not listed here or that do not function as described here.

Table 17. Common options

Option	Description
-D date	Use the most recent revision no later than *date* (see the "Date formats" section for supported date formats).
-f	For commands that involve tags (via -r) or dates (via -D), include files not tagged with the specified tag or not present on the specified date. The most recent revision will be included.
-k kflag	Determine how to perform keyword substitution. The space between -k and kflag is optional. See Table 19 for the list of keyword substitution modes.
-l	Don't recurse into subdirectories.
-n	Don't run module programs.
R	Do recurse into subdirectories (the default). As of Version 1.11, CVS can work in sandboxes with directories checked out from different repositories.
-r rev	Use a particular revision number or symbolic tag.

Table 18 shows which common options are applicable to each user command.

Table 18. Common client option applicability

Command	-D	-f	-k	-l	-n	-R	-r
add			•				
annotate	•	•		•		•	•
checkout	•	•	•	•	•	•	•
commit				•		•	•
diff	•			•		•	•
edit				•		•	
editors				•		•	
export	•	•	•	•	•	•	•
help							

Table 18. Common client option applicability (continued)

Command	-D	-f	-k	-l	-n	-R	-r
history	•						•
import			•				
log				•		•	
login							
logout							
rannotate	•	•		•		•	•
rdiff	•	•		•		•	•
release							
remove				•		•	
rlog				•		•	
rtag	•	•		•		•	•
status				•		•	
tag				•		•	
unedit				•		•	
update	•	•	•	•		•	•
version							
watch				•		•	
watchers				•		•	

Date formats

CVS understands dates in a variety of formats, including:

ISO standard
> The preferred format is YYYY-MM-DD HH:MM, which reads as 2000-05-17, or 2000-05-17 22:00. The technical details of the format are defined in the ISO 8601 standard.

Email standard
> 17 May 2000. The technical details of the format are defined in the RFC-822 and RFC-1123 standards.

Relative
> 10 days ago, 4 years ago.

Common
> *month/day/year*. This form can cause confusion because not all cultures use the first two fields in this order (1/2/2000 would be ambiguous).

Other
> Other formats are accepted, including YYYY/MM/DD and those omitting the year (which is assumed to be the current year).

Keyword substitutions

Table 19 describes the keyword substitution modes that can be selected with the -*k* option. CVS uses keyword substitutions to insert revision information into files when they are checked out or updated.

Table 19. Keyword substitution modes

Mode	Description
b	Binary mode. Treat the file the same as with mode o, but also avoid newline conversion.
k	Keyword-only mode. Flatten all keywords to just the keyword name. Use this mode if you want to compare two revisions of a file without seeing the keyword substitution differences.
kv	Keyword-value mode. The keyword and the corresponding value are substituted. This is the default mode.
kvl	Keyword-value-locker mode. This mode is the same as kv mode, except it always adds the lock holder's user ID if the revision is locked. The lock is obtained via the cvs admin -l command.
o	Old-contents mode. Use the keyword values as they appear in the repository rather than generate new values.
v	Value-only mode. Substitute the value of each keyword for the entire keyword field, omitting even the $ delimiters. This mode destroys the field in the process, so use it cautiously.

Keyword substitution fields are strings of the form $*Keyword* ...$. The valid keywords are:

Author
> The user ID of the person who committed the revision.

Date
> The date and time (in standard UTC format) the revision was committed.

Header
> The full path of the repository RCS file, the revision number; the commit date, time, and user ID; the file's state; and the lock holder's user ID if the file is locked.

Id
> A shorter form of Header, omitting the leading directory name(s) from the RCS file's path, leaving only the filename.

Name
> The tag name that retrieves the file, or empty if no explicit tag was given when the file was retrieved.

Locker
> The user ID of the user holding a lock on the file, or empty if the file is not locked.

Log
> The RCS filename. In addition to keyword expansion in the keyword field, each commit adds additional lines to the file immediately following the line containing this keyword. The first such line contains the revision number and the commit date, time, and user ID. Subsequent lines are the contents of the commit log message. The result over time is a reverse-chronological list of log entries for the file. Each additional line is preceded by the

same characters that precede the keyword field on its
line. This allows the log information to be formatted in a
comment for most languages. For example:

```
#
# foo.pl
#
# $Log: ch01,v $
#
# Revision 1.2   2000/06/09 22:10:23   me
# Fixed the new bug introduced when the last one
# was fixed.
#
# Revision 1.1   2000/06/09 18:07:51   me
# Fixed the last remaining bug in the system.
#
```

Be sure not to place any keyword fields in your log messages if you use this keyword, because CVS will expand
them if you do.

RCSfile
>   The name of the RCS file (without any leading
>   directories).

Revision
>   The revision number of the file.

Source
>   The full path of the RCS file.

State
>   The file's state, as assigned by cvs admin -s (if you don't
>   set the state explicitly, it is Exp by default).

User Commands

The CVS client program provides the user commands
defined in Table 20.

Table 20. User commands

Command	Description
ad add new	Indicate that files/directories should be added to the repository.
ann annotate	Display contents of the head revision of a file, annotated with the revision number, user, and date of the last change for each line.
checkout co get	Create a sandbox for a module.
ci com commit	Commit changes from the sandbox back to the repository.
di dif diff	View differences between file versions.
edit	Prepare to edit files; used for enhanced developer coordination.
editors	Display a list of users working on the files; used for enhanced developer coordination.
ex exp export	Retrieve a module, but don't make the result a sandbox.
help	Get help.
hi his history	Display the log information for files.
im imp import	Import new modules into the repository.
lgn login logon	Log in to (cache the password for) a remote CVS server.
lo log	Show the activity log for the file(s).

Table 20. User commands (continued)

Command	Description
logout	Log off from (flush the password for) a remote CVS server.
pa patch rdiff	Release `diff`; the output is the format of input to Larry Wall's `patch` command; doesn't have to be run from within a sandbox.
rannotate	Display contents of the head revision of a module, annotated with the revision number, user, and date of the last change for each line.
re rel release	Perform a logged delete on a sandbox.
rlog	Show the activity log for the module(s).
remove rm delete	Remove a file or directory from the repository.
rt rtag rfreeze	Tag a particular revision.
st stat status	Show detailed status for files.
ta tag freeze	Attach a tag to files in the repository.
unedit	Abandon file modifications and make read-only again.
up upd update	Synchronize sandbox to repository.
ver version	Display the version of the CVS client (and server, if appropriate) being used.
watch	Manage the watch settings; used for enhanced developer coordination.
watchers	Display the list of users watching for changes to the files; used for enhanced developer coordination.

add

```
add
  [ -k kflag ]
  [ -m message ]
  file ...
```

This command indicates that files/directories should be added to the repository. They are not actually added until they are committed via cvs commit. This command can also resurrect files that have been deleted with cvs remove.

The standard meaning of the common client option -k applies. The only additional option that can be used with the add command is -m message. This option provides a description of the file (which appears in the output of the log command).

annotate

```
annotate
  [ [ -D date | -r rev ] -f ]
  [ -F ]
  [ -l | -R ]
  file ...
```

CVS displays a report showing each line of the specified file. Each line is prefixed by information about the most recent change to the line, including the revision number, user, and date. If no revision is specified, the head revision of the trunk branch is used.

The standard meanings of the common client options -D, -f, -l, -r, and -R apply. The meaning of option -F is listed in Table 21.

Table 21. annotate option

Option	Description
-F	Annotate binary files; CVS normally skips binary files.

checkout

```
checkout
   [ -A ]
   [ -c | -s ]
   [ -d dir [ -N ] ]
   [ [ -D date | -r rev ] -f ]
   [ -j rev1 [ -j rev2 ] ]
   [ -k kflag ]
   [ -l | -R ]
   [ -n ]
   [ -p ]
   [ -P ]
   [ module ... ]
```

This command copies files from the repository to the sandbox. The *module* argument must be omitted when using option -c or option -s. Otherwise, you must list at least one module.

The standard meanings of the common client options -D, -f, -k, -l, -n, -r, and -R apply. Additional options are listed in Table 22.

Table 22. checkout options

Option	Description
-A	Reset any sticky tags or dates.
-c	Display the contents of the *modules* administrative file.
-d dir	Override the default directory name.
-j rev	Join branches together.
-N	Don't shorten module paths.
-p	Pipe the files to standard output, with header lines between them showing the filename, RCS filename, and version.
-P	Prune empty directories.
-s	Show status for each module from the *modules* administrative file.

commit

```
commit
  [ -f | [ -l | -R ] ]
  [ -F file | -m message ]
  [ -n ]
  [ -r revision ]
  [ file ... ]
```

This command commits the changes (if any) made to the specified files in the sandbox to the repository. If no files are specified, commits all modified files.

The standard meanings of the common client options -l, -n, -r, and -R apply. Additional options are listed in Table 23.

Table 23. commit options

Option	Description
-f	Force commit, even if no changes are made.
-F file	Use the contents of the file as the message.
-m message	Use the message specified.

Use of the -r option causes the revision to be "sticky," requiring the use of admin -A to continue to use the sandbox.

diff

```
diff
  [ -k kflag ]
  [ -l | -R ]
  [ format ]
  [ [ -r rev1 | -D date1 ] [ -r rev2 | -D date2 ] ]
  [ file ... ]
```

This command compares two versions of a file and displays the differences in a format determined by the options. By default, the sandbox version of the file is compared to the repository version it was originally copied from.

The standard meanings of the common client options -D, -k, -l, -r, and -R apply. All options for the diff command can also be used.

Table 24 shows some options available with the GNU diff program that are supported by cvs diff. See the GNU diff manual page (man diff) or info page (info diff) for full explanations. If you don't have the GNU version of diff installed, the documentation is available online at *http://www. gnu.org/manual/diffutils-2.7/html_mono/ diff.html* (the GNU web site).

Table 24. diff format options

Option	Description
--binary	Treat the files as binary; has no effect on Unix-like systems, but on systems that use a carriage return followed by a line feed as the line-ending sequence, this option causes the carriage return to be treated like any other character, instead of ignoring it as usual.
--brief	Tell whether or not the files differ, without providing further details.
-c	Use the context output format.
-C nlines --context[= lines]	Show the specified number of lines of context when using context output format.
-t --expand-tabs	Expand tabs to spaces in output.
-w --ignore-all-space	Don't report differences in amount of whitespace, even if one revision has whitespace in a place the other has none.
-B --ignore-blank-lines	Don't report differences in number of blank lines.
-i --ignore-case	Don't report differences in case.
-b --ignore-space-change	Don't report differences in amount of whitespace or whitespace at the end of a line.
-T --initial-tab	Put a tab instead of a space after the indicator character on output, which makes tabs line up correctly in the output.
-d --minimal	Use an alternate algorithm that may find smaller diffs but may take a lot longer to run.
-N --new-file	Treat new files as if a zero-length file were present in the other directory (used for making patches).

Table 24. diff format options (continued)

Option	Description
-n --rcs	Use RCS output format.
-s --report-identical-files	Indicate when two files do not differ.
-p --show-c-function	For C-like languages, show the names of functions in which differences occur.
-y --side-by-side	Show the files side by side.
-a --text	Treat files like text, even if they don't seem to be.
-u --unified[= nlines]	Use the unified diff output format.
-U nlines	Show this many lines of context on unified diff output format.
-V style	Control the style of backup files created.

edit

```
edit
  [ -a action ]
  [ -l | -R ]
  [ file ... ]
```

The edit command is used with watch to permit a more coordinated (serialized) development process. It makes the file writable and sends out an advisory to any users that have requested them. A temporary watch is established and will be removed automatically when either the unedit or the commit command is issued.

The standard meanings of the common client options -l and -R apply. The only additional option that can be used with the edit command is -a actions. This option specifies the actions to watch. The legal values for actions are described in the entry for the watch command.

editors

```
editors
  [ -l | -R ]
  [ file ... ]
```

This command displays a list of users working on the files specified. This is determined by checking which users have run the edit command on those files. If the edit command has not been used, no results are displayed.

The standard meanings of the common client options *-l* and *-R* apply.

See also watch.

export

```
export
  [ -d dir [ -N ] ]
  [ -D date | -r rev ]
  [ -f ]
  [ -k kflag ]
  [ -l | -R ]
  [ -n ]
  [ -P ]
  module ...
```

This command exports files from the repository, much like the checkout command, except that the result is not a sand-box (i.e., CVS subdirectories are not created). You can use this to prepare a directory for distribution. For example:

```
$ cvs export -r foo-1_0 -d foo-1.0 foo
$ tar czf foo-1.0.tar.gz foo-1.0
```

The standard meanings of the common client options *-D*, *-f*, *-k*, *-l*, *-n*, *-r*, and *-R* apply. Additional options are listed in Table 25.

Table 25. export options

Option	Description
-d *dir*	Use *dir* as the directory name instead of using the module name.
-n	Don't run any checkout programs.
-N	Don't shorten paths.

When checking out a single file located one or more directories down in a module's directory structure, the -N option can be used with -d to prevent the creation of intermediate directories.

help

```
help
```

This command displays helpful information about using the cvs program.

history

```
history
    [ -a | -u user ]
    [ -b string ]
    [ -c ]
    [ -D date ]
    [ -e | -x type ]
    [ -f file | -m module | -n module | -p repository ]…
    [ -l ]
    [ -o ]
    [ -r rev ]
    [ -t tag ]
    [ -T ]
    [ -w ]
    [ -x types ]
    [ -z zone ]
    [ file ... ]
```

This command displays historical information. To use the history command, you must first set up the *history* administrative file in the repository. See the "Repository Structure" section for more information on this file.

The standard meanings of the common client options -*D* and -*r* apply. History is reported for activity subsequent to the date or revision indicated. Additional options are listed in Table 26.

Table 26. history options

Option	Description
-*a*	Show history for all users (default is current user).
-*b str*	Show history back to the first record containing str in the module name, filename, or repository path.
-*c*	Report each commit.
-*e*	Report everything.
-*f file*	Show the most recent event for $file$.
-*l*	Show last event only.
-*m module*	Produce a full report on $module$.
n module	Report the last event for $module$.
-*o*	Report on modules that have been checked out.
-*p repository*	Show history for a particular repository directory.
-*t tag*	Show history since tag was last added to the history file.
-*T*	Report on all tags.
-*u name*	Show history for a particular user.
-*w*	Show history only for the current working directory.
-*x types*	Report on specific types of activity; see Table 27.
-*z zone*	Display times according to the specified time zone.

The *-p* option should limit the history report to entries for the directory or directories (if multiple *-p* options are specified) given, but as of Version 1.11.2, it doesn't seem to affect the output. For example, to report history for the *CVSROOT* and *hello* modules, run the command:

```
$ cvs history -p CVSROOT -p hello
```

Using *-t* is faster than using *-r* because it searches only the history file, not all of the RCS files.

The record types shown in Table 27 are generated by *update* commands.

Table 27. update-related history record types

Type	Description
C	Merge was necessary, but conflicts requiring manual intervention occurred.
G	Successful automatic merge.
U	Working file copied from repository.
W	Working copy deleted.

The record types shown in Table 28 are generated by commit commands.

Table 28. commit-related history record types

Type	Description
A	Added for the first time.
M	Modified.
R	Removed.

Each record type shown in Table 29 is generated by a different command.

Table 29. Other history record types

Type	Command
E	export
F	release
O	checkout
T	rtag

import

```
import
    [ -b branch ]
    [ -d ]
    [ -I pattern ]
    [ -k kflag ]
    [ -m message ]
    [ -W spec ]
    module
    vendor_tag
    release_tag ...
```

This command imports an entire directory into the repository as a new module. It incorporates code from outside sources or other code that was initially created outside the control of the CVS repository. More than one *release_tag* may be specified, in which case multiple symbolic tags are created for the initial revision.

The *vendor_tag* argument tracks third-party code that may be used in your project. Using different values for this argument, you can track third-party code separately and upgrade that portion of your code to a new release with a subsequent cvs import command. Because the argument is not optional, you should use some conventional value such as vendor whenever the code being imported shouldn't be tracked separately.

The *release_tag* argument associates a symbolic tag with the initial version of every file being imported. Because this argument is not optional, you should use some conventional value such as start whenever you don't have a more meaningful value to provide. The standard meaning of the common client option -*k* applies. Additional options are listed in Table 30.

Table 30. import options

Option	Description
-*b branch*	Import to a vendor branch.
-*d*	Use the modification date and time of the file instead of the current date and time as the import date and time. For local repository locators only.
-*I pattern*	Filename patterns for files to ignore.
-*m message*	Use *message* as the log message instead of invoking the editor.
-*W spec*	Wrapper specification.

The -*k* setting applies only to files imported during this execution of the command. The keyword substitution modes of files already in the repository are not modified. When used with -*W*, the *spec* variable is in the same format as entries in the *cvswrappers* administrative file (see the "The cvswrappers file" section, earlier in the book).

Table 31 describes the status codes displayed by the import command.

Table 31. import status codes

Status	Description
C	Changed; the file is in the repository, and the sandbox version is different; a merge is required.
I	Ignored; the *.cvsignore* file is causing CVS to ignore the file.
L	Link; symbolic links are ignored by CVS.
N	New; the file is new, and it has been added to the repository.
U	Update; the file is in the repository, and the sandbox version is not different.

log

```
log
   [ -b ]
   [ -d dates ]
   [ -h ]
   [ -N ]
   [ -rrevisions ]
   [ -R ]
   [ -s states ]
   [ -t ]
   [ -wlogins ]
   [ file ... ]
```

This command displays an activity log for the files.

The standard meaning of the common client option *-l* applies. Additional options are listed in Table 32.

Table 32. log options

Option	Description
-b	List revisions on default branch.
d dates	Report on these dates.
-h	Display header only.
-N	Don't display tags.
r[revisions]	Report on the listed revisions. There is no space between -r and its argument. Without an argument, the latest revision of the default branch is used.
-R	Display RCS filename only. The usage of -R here is different from elsewhere in CVS (-R usually causes CVS to operate recursively).
-s states	Display only those revisions having one of the specified states.
-S	Don't display the header if the output would otherwise be empty.
-t	Display only header and descriptive text.
-w logins	Report on checkins by the listed logins. There is no space between -w and its argument.

For -*d*, use the date specifications in Table 33. Multiple specifications separated by semicolons may be provided. For -*s*, separate multiple states with commas.

Table 33. log date range specifications

Specification	Description
d1<*d2* or *d2*>*d1*	The revisions dated between *d1* and *d2*, exclusive.
d1<=*d2* or *d2*>=*d1*	The revisions dated between *d1* and *d2*, inclusive.
<*d* or *d*>	The revisions dated before *d*.
<=*d* or *d*>=	The revisions dated on or before *d*.
d< or >*d*	The revisions dated after *d*.
d<= or >=*d*	The revisions dated on or after *d*.
d	The most recent revision dated *d* or earlier.

For -*r*, use the revision specifications in Table 34.

Table 34. log revision specifications

Specification	Description
rev1:rev2	The revisions between *rev1* and *rev2*, inclusive.
:*rev*	The revisions from the beginning of the branch to *rev*, inclusive.
rev:	The revisions from *rev* to the end of the branch, inclusive.
branch	All revisions on the branch.
branch1:branch2	All revisions on all branches between *branch1* and *branch2*, inclusive.
branch.	The latest revision on the branch.

For *rev1:rev2*, it is an error if the revisions are not on the same branch.

login

```
login
```

This command logs in to a remote repository. The password entered is cached in the ~/.cvspass file because a connection to the server is not maintained across invocations.

logout

```
logout
```

This command logs out of a remote repository. The password cached in the ~/.cvspass file is deleted.

rannotate

```
rannotate
   [ [ -D date | -r rev ] -f ]
   [ -F ]
   [ -l | -R ]
   module ...
```

This command displays a report showing each line of the specified module or module file. Each line is prefixed by information about the most recent change to the line, including the revision number, user, and date. If no revision is specified, the head of the trunk is used.

The rannotate command differs from the annotate command in that it refers directly to modules (and their files) in the repository rather than inferring the module based on the sandbox from which it is run. The first path component of each module argument must be a valid module for the repository.

The standard meanings of the common client options -D, -f, -l, -r, and -R apply. Table 35 lists an additional option.

Table 35. rannotate option

Option	Description
-F	Annotate binary files; CVS normally skips binary files.

rdiff

```
rdiff
    [ -c | -s | -u ]
    [ { { -D date1 | -r rev1 } [ -D date2 | -r rev2 ] } | -t ]
    [ -f ]
    [ -l | -R ]
    [-V vn]
    file ...
```

This command creates a patch file that can convert a directory containing one release to a different release.

The standard meanings of the common client options -D, -f, -l, -r, and -R apply. Additional options are listed in Table 36.

Table 36. rdiff options

Option	Description
-c	Use context diff format (the default).
-s	Output a summary of changed files instead of a patch file.
-t	Show the differences between the two most recent revisions.
-u	Use unified diff (unidiff) format.
-V rcsver	Obsolete; used to specify version of RCS to emulate for keyword expansion (keyword expansion emulates RCS Version 5).

release

```
release
    [ -d ]
    directory ...
```

Sandboxes can be abandoned or deleted without using cvs release; using the release command logs an entry to the history file (if this mechanism is configured) about the sandbox being destroyed. In addition, it checks the disposition (recursively) of each sandbox file before deleting anything. This helps prevent destroying work that has not yet been committed.

There is only one option that can be used with the release command, -d. The -d option deletes the sandbox copy if no uncommitted changes are present.

TIP

New directories in the sandbox (and the files they contain) are deleted if the -d option is used with release.

The status codes listed in Table 37 describe the disposition of each file encountered in the repository and the sandbox.

Table 37. release status codes

Status	Description
A	The sandbox file has been added (the file was created and cvs add was run), but the addition has not been committed.
M	The sandbox copy of the file has been modified.
P U	Update available. There is a newer version of the file in the repository, and the copy in the sandbox has not been modified.
R	The sandbox copy was removed (the file was deleted and cvs remove was run), but the removal was not committed.
?	The file is present in the sandbox but not in the repository.

remove

```
remove
    [ -f ]
    [ -l | -R ]
    [ file ... ]
```

This command indicates that files should be removed from the repository. The files aren't removed until they are committed. Use cvs add to resurrect files that have been removed if you change your mind later.

The standard meanings of the common client options -l and -R apply. Only one other option is used with the remove command, -f. When used, -f deletes the file from the sandbox first.

rlog

```
rlog
    [ -b ]
    [ -d dates ]
```

```
[ -h ]
[ -N ]
[ -rrevisions ]
[ -R ]
[ -s state ]
[ -t ]
[ -wlogins ]
[ module ... ]
```

This command displays an activity log for the modules.

The standard meaning of the common client option *-l* applies. Additional options are listed in Table 38.

Table 38. rlog options

Option	Description
-b	List revisions on default branch.
-d dates	Report on these dates.
-h	Display header only.
-N	Don't display tags.
-r[revisions]	Report on the listed revisions. There is no space between *-r* and its argument. Without an argument, the latest revision of the default branch is used.
-R	Display RCS filename only. The usage of *-R* here is different from elsewhere in CVS (*-R* usually causes CVS to operate recursively).
-s state	Display only those revisions having the specified state.
-t	Display only header and descriptive text.
-w logins	Report on checkins by the listed logins. There is no space between *-w* and its argument.

For *-d*, use the date specifications in Table 33. Multiple specifications separated by semicolons may be provided.

For *-r*, use the revision specifications in Table 34.

rtag

```
rtag
    [ -a ]
    [ -b ]
```

```
[ -B ]
[ -d ]
[ -D date | -r rev ]
[ -f ]
[ -F ]
[ -l | - R ]
[ -n ]
tag
file ...
```

This command assigns a tag to a particular revision of a set of files. If the file already uses the tag for a different revision, cvs rtag complains unless the -F option is used. This command doesn't refer to the sandbox file revisions (use cvs tag for that), so it can be run outside a sandbox, if desired.

The standard meanings of the common client options -D, -f, -l, -r, and -R apply. Additional options are listed in Table 39.

Table 39. rtag options

Option	Description
-a	Search the *Attic* directory for removed files containing the tag.
-b	Make it a branch tag.
-B	Allow movement or deletion of branch tags (used with -d or -F).
-d	Delete the tag.
-F	Force; move the tag from its current revision to the one specified.
-n	Don't run any tag program from the *modules* file.

status

```
status
  [ -l | -R ]
  [ -v ]
  [ file ... ]
```

This command displays the status of the files.

The standard meanings of the common client options -l and -R apply. You can use status -v to include tag information.

tag

```
tag
  [ -b ]
  [ -c ]
  [ -d ]
  [ -D date | -r rev ]
  [ -f ]
  [ -F ]
  [ -l | R ]
  tag
  [ file ... ]
```

This command assigns a tag to the sandbox revisions of a set of files. You can use the status -v command to list the existing tags for a file.

The *tag* must start with a letter and consist entirely of letters, numbers, dashes and underscores. Therefore, while you might want to tag your *hello* project with 1.0 when you release Version 1.0, you must tag it with something like hello-1_0 instead.

The standard meanings of the common client options -D, -f, -l, -r, and -R apply. Additional options are listed in Table 40.

Table 40. tag options

Option	Description
-b	Make a branch.
-c	Check for changes; make sure the files aren't locally modified before tagging.
-d	Delete the tag.
-F	Force; move the tag from its current revision to the one specified.

Because the -d option throws away information that might be important, you should use it only when absolutely necessary. It is usually better to create a different tag with a similar name.

unedit

```
unedit
  [ -l | -R ]
  [ file ... ]
```

This command abandons file modifications and makes the file read-only again. Watchers are notified.

The standard meanings of the common client options -l and -R apply.

update

```
update
  [ -A ]
  [ -C ]
  [ -d ]
  [ -D date | -r rev ]
  [ -f ]
  [ -I pattern ]
  [ -j rev1 [ -j rev2 ] ]
  [ -k kflag ]
  [ -l | -R ]
  [ -p ]
  [ -P ]
  [ -W spec ]
  [ file ... ]
```

This command updates the sandbox, merging in any changes from the repository. For example:

```
$ cvs -n -q update -AdP
```

does a quick status check of the current sandbox versus the head revision of the trunk branch of development.

The standard meanings of the common client options -D, -f, -k, -l, -r, and -R apply. Additional options are listed in Table 41.

Table 41. update options

Option	Description
-A	Reset sticky tags.
-C	Replace modified files with clean copies.

Table 41. update options (continued)

Option	Description
-d	Create and update new directories.
-I *pattern*	Provide filename patterns for files to ignore.
-j *revision*	Merge in (join) changes between two revisions.
-p	Check out files to standard output.
-P	Prune empty directories.
-W *spec*	Provide wrapper specification.

When using -C, CVS makes backups of modified files before copying the clean version. The backup files are named .#file.revision.

Using -D or -r results in sticky dates or tags, respectively, on the affected files (using -p along with these prevents stickiness). Use -A to reset any sticky tags or dates.

If two -j specifications are made, the differences between them are computed and applied to the current file. If only one is given, the common ancestor of the sandbox revision and the specified revision are used as a basis for computing differences to be merged. For example, suppose a project has an experimental branch, and important changes to the file *foo.c* are introduced between revisions 1.2.2.1 and 1.2.2.2. Once those changes prove stable, you want them reflected in the main line of development. From a sandbox with the head revisions checked out, run:

```
$ cvs update -j 1.2.2.1 -j 1.2.2.2 foo.c
```

CVS finds the differences between the two revisions and applies those differences to the file in your sandbox.

The *spec* used with -W is in the same format as entries in the *cvswrappers* administrative file (see the "The cvswrappers file" section).

The status codes listed in Table 42 describe the action taken on each file encountered in the repository and the sandbox.

Table 42. update status codes

Status code	Description
A	Added. Server took no action because there was no repository file. Indicates that `cvs add`, but not `cvs commit`, has been run.
C	Conflict. Sandbox copy is modified (it has been edited since it was checked out or last committed). There was a new revision in the repository, and there were conflicts when CVS merged its changes into the sandbox version.
M	Modified. Sandbox copy is modified (it has been edited since it was checked out or last committed). If there was a new revision in the repository, its changes were successfully merged into the file (no conflicts).
P	Patched. Same as U (updated) but indicates the server used a patch.
R	Removed. Server took no action. Indicates that `cvs remove`, but not `cvs commit`, has been run.
U	Updated. The file was brought up to date.
?	File is present in sandbox but not in repository.

version

```
version
```

This command displays the version of the CVS client (and server, if appropriate) being used.

watch

```
watch
    { { on | off } | { add | remove } [ -a action ] }
    [ -l | -R ]
    file ...
```

The watch command controls CVS's edit tracking mechanism. By default, CVS operates in its concurrent development mode, allowing any user to edit any file at any time. CVS includes this watch mechanism to support developers who would rather be notified of edits made by others proactively than discover them when doing an update. The *CVSROOT/notify* file determines how notifications are performed.

Table 43 shows the watch subcommands and their uses.

Table 43. watch subcommands

Subcommand	Description
add	Start watching files.
off	Turn off watching.
on	Turn on watching.
remove	Stop watching files.

The standard meanings of the common client options -*l* and -*R* apply. The only other option that can be used with the watch command is -*a action*. The -*a* option is used with one of the actions listed in Table 44.

Table 44. watch actions

Action	Description
all	All of the following.
commit	A user has committed changes.
edit	A user ran cvs edit.
none	Don't watch; used by the edit command.
unedit	A user ran cvs unedit, cvs release, or deleted the file and ran cvs update, recreating it.

See also edit, editors, unedit, and watchers.

watchers

```
watchers
  [ -l | -R ]
  [ file ... ]
```

This command displays a list of users watching the specified files. This is determined by checking which users have run the watch command on a particular file (or set of files). If the watch command has not been used, no results are displayed.

The standard meanings of the common client options *-l* and *-R* apply. See also watch.

Related Resources

There are many CVS-related programs freely available on the Internet. This section references a few of them.

Emacs CVS Mode

GNU Emacs (*http://www.gnu.org/software/emacs/emacs.html*) has a built-in mode (called VC Mode) for working with CVS. See *GNU Emacs Pocket Reference* by Debra Cameron (O'Reilly) for more information.

Perl

The following Perl script can build solutions around CVS:

cvs2cl.pl
> Converts CVS log messages to GNU-style ChangeLog entries; by Karl Fogel
>
> *http://www.red-bean.com/cvs2cl*

CVS Clients

The CVS distribution includes a complete command-line client implementation. In addition, there are many graphical client programs for accessing CVS repositories:

Cervisia
> A CVS frontend for *KDE* (*http://www.kde.org*)
>
> *http://cervisia.sourceforge.net*

KDevelop
>   An Integrated Development Environment for KDE with a
>   built-in CVS client
>
>   *http://www.kdevelop.org/*

LinCVS
>   A graphical Linux and Windows CVS client written with
>   the Qt toolkit
>
>   *http://www.trolltech.com/products/qt/*

pcl-cvs
>   An Emacs dired-like CVS mode by Stefan Monnier
>
>   *ftp://rum.cs.yale.edu/pub/monnier/pcl-cvs*

Pharmacy
>   A CVS frontend for *GNOME* (*http://www.gnome.org*)
>
>   *http://pharmacy.sourceforge.net/*

CvsGui
>   CVS clients for Linux (gCvs), Microsoft Windows
>   (WinCvs), and Macintosh (MacCvs)
>
>   *http://cvsgui.sourceforge.net*

CVS Utilities

The following programs automate common activities with
CVS:

cvsadmin
>   A simple program to administor users of a CVS reposi-
>   tory, including adding and removing users and setting
>   and changing passwords
>
>   *http://www.cooptel.qc.ca/~limitln/cvsadmin/*

ltag
>   A program that lists the symbolic tags appearing any-
>   where within or below a CVS sandbox directory
>
>   *http://www.focusresearch.com/gregor/ltag/*

CVS Web Interfaces

These CVS client interfaces allow you to view the contents of a repository with a web browser:

bonzai
> A Perl- and MySQL-based web interface to CVS repositories; part of the Mozilla project
>
> *http://www.mozilla.org/projects/bonsai/*

chora
> A PHP-based web interface to CVS repositories by Chuck Hagenbuch and Anil Madhavapeddy
>
> *http://www.horde.org/chora/*

CVSweb
> A Perl- and CGI based web interface to CVS repositories by Bill Fenner, Henner Zeller, Akinori Musha, Ville Skyttä, et al.
>
> *http://www.freebsd.org/projects/cvsweb.html*

ViewCVS
> A Python- and CGI-based web interface to CVS repositories by Greg Stein
>
> *http://viewcvs.sourceforge.net/*

Index

We'd like to hear your suggestions for improving our indexes. Send email to
index@oreilly.com.

W

X

Related Titles Available from O'Reilly

Unix Administration

DNS & BIND, *4th Edtion*

DNS & BIND Cookbook

Essential CVS

Essential System
Administration, *3rd Edition*

Essential System
Administration Pocket Reference

Postfix: The Definitive Guide

qmail

sendmail, *3rd Edition*

sendmail Cookbook

System Performance Tuning,
2nd Edition

The Unix CD Bookshelf,
Version 3.0

Unix Backup & Recovery

Unix Basics

GNU Emacs Pocket Reference

Learning GNU Emacs,
2nd Edition

Learning the bash Shell,
2nd Edition

Learning the Korn Shell

Learning the Unix
Operating System,
5th Edition

Learning the vi Editor, *6th
Edition*

sed & awk Pocket Reference,
2nd Edition

sed & awk, *2nd Edition*

Unix in a Nutshell,
System V Edition,
3rd Edition

Using csh & tcsh

Unix Tools

Effective awk Programming,
3rd Edition

lex & yacc, *2nd Edition*

Managing Projects with make,
2nd Edition

Practical PostgreSQL

The Complete FreeBSD,
4th Edition

Unix Power Tools, *3rd Edition*

Writing GNU Emacs
Extensions

O'REILLY®

Our books are available at most retail and online bookstores.
To order direct: 1-800-998-9938 • *order@oreilly.com* • *www.oreilly.com*
Online editions of most O'Reilly titles are available at *safari.oreilly.com*

Keep in touch with O'Reilly

1. Download examples from our books

To find example files for a book, go to:
www.oreilly.com/catalog

select the book, and follow the "Examples" link.

2. Register your O'Reilly books

Register your book at *register.oreilly.com*

Why register your books? Once you've registered your O'Reilly books you can:

- Win O'Reilly books, T-shirts or discount coupons in our monthly drawing.
- Get special offers available only to registered O'Reilly customers.
- Get catalogs announcing new books (US and UK only).
- Get email notification of new editions of the O'Reilly books you own.

3. Join our email lists

Sign up to get topic-specific email announcements of new books and conferences, special offers, and O'Reilly Network technology newsletters at:
elists.oreilly.com

It's easy to customize your free elists subscription so you'll get exactly the O'Reilly news you want.

4. Get the latest news, tips, and tools
www.oreilly.com

- "Top 100 Sites on the Web"—PC Magazine
- CIO Magazine's Web Business 50 Awards

Our web site contains a library of comprehensive product information (including book excerpts and tables of contents), downloadable software, background articles, interviews with technology leaders, links to relevant sites, book cover art, and more.

5. Work for O'Reilly

Check out our web site for current employment opportunities:
jobs.oreilly.com

6. Contact us

O'Reilly & Associates, Inc.
1005 Gravenstein Hwy North
Sebastopol, CA 95472 USA

TEL: 707-827-7000 or 800-998-9938
        (6am to 5pm PST)

FAX: 707-829-0104

order@oreilly.com
> For answers to problems regarding your order or our products.
> To place a book order online, visit:
> *www.oreilly.com/order_new*

catalog@oreilly.com
> To request a copy of our latest catalog.

booktech@oreilly.com
> For book content technical questions or corrections.

corporate@oreilly.com
> For educational, library, government, and corporate sales.

proposals@oreilly.com
> To submit new book proposals to our editors and product managers.

international@oreilly.com
> For information about our international distributors or translation queries. For a list of our distributors outside of North America check out:
> *international.oreilly.com/distributors.html*

adoption@oreilly.com
> For information about academic use of O'Reilly books, visit:
> *academic.oreilly.com*

O'REILLY®

Our books are available at most retail and online bookstores.
To order direct: 1-800-998-9938 • *order@oreilly.com* • *www.oreilly.com*
Online editions of most O'Reilly titles are available at *safari.oreilly.com*